ART TREASURES OF ASIA

GENERAL EDITOR: JANE GASTON MAHLER

PERSIAN MINIATURES

THE STORY OF RUSTAM

Edited, with Introduction and Notes, by

William Lillys

CHARLES E. TUTTLE COMPANY

RUTLAND, VERMONT & TOKYO, JAPAN

Contents

First edition, 1958. All rights reserved
Library of Congress Catalog Card No. 58-13429
Text printed by the Kenkyusha Printing Co., Tokyo. Color plates engraved and
printed by the Mitsumura Color Printing Co., Tokyo. Manufactured in Japan

Introduction

by William Lillys

BEGINNING in legendary antiquity the *Shahnama* or "Book of Kings" sweeps across ages of Persian civilization in an epic poem of some 60,000 verses by the 10th-century poet Firdausi. Its stream of events traces the fortunes of heroes and kings, telling of their exploits and splendor, their vast armies and devastating wars.

Many of these events are brought to vivid reality in illustrated editions of the *Shahnama*. The artists who were commissioned by princely patrons to highlight exquisitely written texts with miniatures, contributed to an art of unsurpassed brilliance. Using radiant mineral colors, applied to the finest polished papers, and delicate brushes for outlines, the Iranian genius fashioned paintings of richness and power equal to the poet's imagery. Whether rendered with bold simplicity or intricate detail they always maintain a clarity and decorative surface in harmony with the fine calligraphy of the page. Though intended primarily as book illustrations, these pictures can, and often do, stand on their own merits as enduring works of art. With moods that vary as the situations demand, some capture the tender, transient emotions of intimacy, others the more monumental flashes of battle and heroism. In the *Shahnama* we witness the life-cycles of great empires and leaders; through the miniature paintings we experience their most dramatic moments.

Of the many dramas that unfold from this immense and complex narrative, few have captured the Persian imagination as much as the story of Rustam. This most extraordinary of heroes, a major figure in the early or mythical period of the epic, was destined from birth to be the guardian and sometimes savior of the Iranian people. Throughout his life's span of some six hundred years Rustam remained a paragon of justice, courage, and, except for one notable instance,[1] of fidelity to his king and country.

No less than eight shahs ruled over Iran during Rustam's lifetime, many of them indebted to his remarkable services for their retention of the throne. Firdausi often reminds us of Rustam's gigantic physical stature by comparing him with the size of an elephant. So great was his strength, too, that Rustam prayed for God to diminish it in order to live among mankind without causing unintended destruction. In many respects he represented a heroic ideal although by no means total perfection. As a semi-divine being, Rustam was subject to some earthly weaknesses and to the inescapable forces of destiny that often placed him in positions of great moral conflict. Far from being the crafty plotter, his role was essentially that of avenger and deliverer, an active agent of the "light principle" which, in Zoroastrian philosophy, stands for purity and good in opposition to the "dark principle" or evil. In the face of unending conflict with the forces of darkness, and even against the more princely hero, Isfandiyar,[2] Rustam consistently upheld his principles of righteousness to the very last.

Because they provided almost unlimited opportunity to depict a wide range of situations, Rustam's exploits were a favorite subject with manuscript illustrators. One of the earliest paintings of an incident concerning Rustam appears, not in a book, but on a 12th-century pottery goblet. Little of the manuscript illustration of the Saljuk period (1037–1194 A.D.) is known today, but the painting of that time has survived in the decoration on polychrome or "Minai" ware from Rayy and Kashan. The narrative painting shown in Figure 1 tells the story of Bizhan and Manizha (see page 12). Mesopotamian manuscript painting of a century later, similar in appearance, indicates the possibility that these artists based their style upon Persian Saljuk models. Sometimes referred to as the "Baghdad School," the painters of this region used highly conventionalized forms in rather naive decorative schemes. Color was

[1] See text to Plate VII.

[2] See text to Plates VII and VIII.

3

brilliant mineral pigment, usually applied in flat areas and enhanced by touches of gold. The boldness of the drawing, though lacking the refinement of later work, had an essential vigor that was to survive in the best productions of the mature Timurid (1370–1500) and Safavid (1502–1736) periods.

Chinese art, long admired by the Persians, came into prominence along with the invasions by Ghenghis Khan and his Mongol tribes from Central Asia. The Il-Khan dynasty which they established in 1256 brought into West Asia many artists and craftsmen from the Far East. Chinese ink painting of the Sung (960–1279) and Yüan (1260–1368) dynasties, thus becoming better known in Iran, had a remarkable effect on the native painting. Greater attention was given to the beauty and flow of pure line and less to color. Like their Mongol cousins in Yüan China, the Il-Khans were foreign rulers over a superior culture who saw fit to perpetuate the indigenous arts rather than attempt to impose what they had of their own. The Persian khans, therefore, encouraged the artists in their court libraries to copy and illustrate literature of national importance – the *Shahnama* included.

One of the finest *Shahnama*'s of the Il-Khan period, probably made around the mid-1300's, is called the "Demotte" manuscript after the name of the last owner, who dispersed its leaves into collections in Europe and America. Probably begun for the last of the Il-Khanid rulers, Abu Sa'id, at the Tabriz art center, some fifty-five illustrations were produced for this book by two or more painters whose identity is still a matter of controversy. Two styles are clearly in evidence here; one is in the Chinese calligraphic manner, the other in the more decorative Persian style. All are unusually large, with figures often nearly filling the pictorial space. (Plates VII, VIII, and IX). With its grandeur of movement and turbulent forms this manuscript conveys a true sense of the epic, marking it an artistic achievement of major importance. Other *Shahnama*'s of this period, in contrast to the "Demotte," have more the quality of the true miniature, the dimensions of the page being smaller and the pictures subordinated to the text (Plates I and IV). In southern Iran the artists of Shiraz continued pre-Mongol traditions. Isolated as it was from the more advanced art center in the north, Shiraz painting of this period is less sophisticated in pictorial conception and technique

and shows fewer elements of Chinese inspiration than the painting from Baghdad and Tabriz.

The late 14th century witnessed another wave of invasion by Mongols from the interior of Asia. This time the entire area from the Euphrates to lands east of the Indus came under the rule of Timur, better known as Tamerlane (1336–1405), who claimed descent from Ghenghis Khan. The eastern provinces of Iran were the most firmly established under the Timurid dynasty, and such cities as Herat, Samarkand, and Shiraz became important centers of artistic activity. From them emerged a new painting style and the flowering of the Persian genius. In the court libraries of the Timurid princes many painters, calligraphers, illuminators, and binders collaborated in the production of magnificent books. The tendency to stress pattern now took precedence over the Far Eastern linearity of a century earlier. This patterning stemmed from the pre-Mongol painting of the Saljuk and "Baghdad School," but it had become subtle and intricate, the color and drawing greatly refined with more elaborate detail (Plate II). Then in the late 15th century, just before the reign of the Safavid shahs, further stylistic developments were introduced and continued into the 16th and 17th centuries. Kamal al-Din Bihzad, unique among Persian painters, added new realism, an expressiveness of feature and gesture, and greater complexity of composition. The Safavid painters Sultan Muhammad, Mir Musavvir, and Mir Sayyid 'Ali further increased the richness and elegance of line and color. The page took on a more pronounced decorative quality with the painting often separated from the text on a page of its own.

Book production began to decline in the late 16th century. The *Shahnama* and other poems were still being illustrated but much attention was now given to creating pictures without reference to literature. Western influence, especially from Italian painting, was increasingly perceptible during the 17th century, with interest growing in the fields of genre and portraiture. The style of the late-16th-century painter, Aqa Riza, noted for grace rather than vitality, was perpetuated into the 17th and 18th centuries, when dazzling color was replaced by delicate tonality and epic theme by mystic speculation and pervading melancholy.

When the Persian Sasanian dynasty fell to the Arab invaders in the 7th century A.D., Iran lost her

Figure 1. GOBLET WITH POLYCHROME DECORATION
Rayy, Saljuk Period, 13th century. h. 4 3/4"
Courtesy of the Smithsonian Institution, Freer Gallery of Art, Washington, D. C.

former identity as a great world power and was absorbed into the Islamic community. About 999, the conqueror Mahmud, an ardent Muslim of Turkic descent, succeeded to his father's throne of Ghazni (now Afghanistan) and went on to take eastern Iran and part of India. At this time, the poet Firdausi was in his sixties and had been at work on his *Shahnama* over twenty years. He was born about the year 935 in a suburb of the city of Tus in Khorasan, the son of an Iranian landowner. His name was Abu'l Kasim Mansur but after he was established as a poet under Mahmud's patronage he

was given the name Firdausi. Although nothing is known of his early training and education, it is certain that he was proficient in the historical and literary traditions of Iran.

Stories of ancient wars and heroes, the struggles and glories of a succession of Iranian dynasties had been handed down for centuries. But it was not until the enlightened reign of the Sasanian monarch Khusrau or Chosroes I (531–79) that a systematic attempt had been made to collect them from all over the empire. Later, these tales and legends were expanded by a group of scholars, one of whom is

5

known as the Dikhan Danishwar, and presented in a Pahlavi or Middle Persian work called the *Khvatai-namak* or "Book of Sovereigns."

Surviving the invasions of the Caliph Omar, the book was preserved and translated into Arabic in the 9th century. Under the Saffarid and succeeding Samanid rulers of the 9th and 10th centuries, the work was continued. The Samanid prince Nuh II, who acceded to the throne in 976, gave it to the poet Dakiki to put into verse. Dakiki was mysteriously murdered shortly after having begun, thereby giving Firdausi the opportunity to realize his own ambition of incorporating this material into an epic poem. In his thirty-sixth year he began to fulfil his dream with the encouragement and patronage of the governor of Tus. However, the poet was determined to dedicate the work to a king and sought Mahmud's support soon after he had attained the Ghaznavid throne. He was heartened at first by a friend at court but palace intrigues delayed royal favor until, after years of waiting and disappointment, the shah finally received him into his household. By 1010, after some thirty years of labor, the *Shahnama* was completed, but, again because of intrigue, Mahmud paid the aging poet far less than had been promised. In revenge, Firdausi ridiculed his patron publicly and then fled to safety. By the time Mahmud was prevailed upon to pay the balance of his debt, the poet was in his eighties. It is said that the shah's gold reached the gates of Tus just as Firdausi's body was being borne to its grave.

Mahmud encouraged the writing of the *Shahnama* despite his being a descendant of the Turkmen or "Turanians" who are described in the poem as Iran's most hated enemies. The Turanians were a legendary rather than an actual nation, a composite foe whose king Afrasiyab was created by the Supreme Evil to destroy Iran. Like the Gog and Magog, they were a fierce barbarian horde, a people of obscure origin who inhabited the fringes of the known world. Although Iran suffered a multitude of invasions from all of her neighbors, the Turkic tribes from out of Central Asia always remained a persistent threat and were, therefore, most directly identified with the Turanians in the *Shahnama*.

The task of reconciling the use of ancient Persian religious names and beliefs with those of Islam, prevailing in 11th-century Iran, was undoubtedly one of Firdausi's most delicate problems, especially since he risked offending his patron, the very orthodox Mahmud. In consequence, the poet made relatively infrequent use of Zoroastrian names, often substituting Moslem equivalents while still keeping the concepts of Zoroastrian dualism in principle. The entire poem is pervaded by the unceasing efforts of the kingdom of darkness to invade and subdue the kingdom of light. The ancient Persian principle of light and good, Hormuzd (Ahura Mazda), is represented upon earth by the Iranians, and Ahriman, the principle of darkness and evil, is personified by the foe of Iran, especially by the Turanians. Although the characters in the poem frequently call upon "God," the name "Hormuzd" is seldom mentioned. Ahriman is called by name more often, as is his Mohammedan counterpart "Iblis," but reference is most frequently made to the *divs*, or fiends and devils, sent by Ahriman to harrass Iran. The two great principles, Hormuzd and Ahriman, rarely appear directly in the *Shahnama*. Each has his intervening agents; the angel Surush and the fabulous bird Simurg appear for the former, and the *divs*, dragons, sorcerers, and witches for the latter.

As in all legend, the *Shahnama* is inconsistent with regard to exact chronology and attaches immense importance to the significance of omens, presentiments, dreams, and the like. Rustam, for example, lives on for centuries and only toward the end of his career is one aware that he has begun to age. Other characters disappear and even die, only to reappear later, young and vigorous as ever, as though there had been no previous or unusual interruption.

As the story begins, Iran was invaded by idolatrous peoples of Arabia and Assyria and ruled by Zahhak (or Dahhak). When Faridun, the Indo-European, recovered Iran from the idolators he divided the world among his three sons. Salm was given the western branch of Indo-Europeans, Iraj the Aryan or Iranian, and Tur inherited the Turanian lands. Iraj was subsequently murdered by his brothers, thus creating a feud in which the struggles with the Turanian element became the most serious. It is noteworthy that Rustam actually represents both the lineages of Faridun and Zahhak as a result of his father's marriage with the daughter of an idolator. His native province of Sistan was renowned for having produced many famous warriors, of whom his father Zal and grandfather Sam were the most honored in Iran and the most feared by the enemy.

The extraordinary circumstances that surrounded the births of Zal and Rustam foretold what unusual personages they would become. Zal was born with white hair. Sam, assuming this unusual quality to be an omen of evil and fearing ridicule at court, had the infant taken out in the wilderness and left to perish. But the fabulous bird Simurg found and nurtured him and, later, when Sam sought for his son, she gave the youth one of her feathers, which he was to burn whenever her protection was needed.

Even more unusual conditions attended the birth of Rustam. His mother, Rudaba, carried him well past the normal time for delivery, suffering many sleepless nights with unceasing pain. Then one day, no longer able to bear her anguish, she fell into a faint. Her husband, Zal, desperately called for the help of his heavenly protector, the fabulous bird Simurg, and received instruction in delivering the child. First the bird ordered Rudaba put into a stupor with wine, in effect to anesthetize her. Then Zal was to give a sharp blade of steel to a priest, who cut open her side and removed the child. Following this, the Simurg showed them how to sew the wound together, dress and anoint it, and, by rubbing one of her magic feathers over it, give it power to heal quickly. The Caesarian delivery, unusual though it may have been, was given increased significance by the assistance of God's agent. The name, Rustam, given the baby referred to the bearing of fruit, symbolizing, therefore, the fulfilment of great promise. Rustam's enormous size at birth was a thing of such wonder that a replica of him was made of stuffed silk and sent to the hero Sam to announce his grandson's arrival. Sam marvelled at Rustam and, foreseeing the power he would wield, admonished both father and son:

"... be just and loyal to the Shahs,
Preferring wisdom over wealth, refraining
Thy hands from evil all thy years, and seeking
God's way from day to day...."[3]

These words, once instilled in him, were to become the fountainhead of Rustam's creed and the basis for his future actions.

Rustam first displayed his incredible strength when he was still no more than a boy. One night he

[3] All quotations and excerpts from the poem are from: A. G. Warner and E. Warner: *The Shahnama of Firdausi*, vols. I–V, London, 1905–25.

was awakened by screams coming from the city: Zal's white elephant had broken free and was running wild through the streets menacing the inhabitants. Rustam grabbed his mace and rushed to the city gates. The guards refused to let him pass through and ridiculed the brash demonstration of courage from so green a youth. This provoked such fury in Rustam that he struck the guards down, broke through the gates and faced the maddened beast alone. Thinking the boy would be easy prey the elephant rushed at him, but as it reared to strike with its trunk, Rustam gave it a single crushing blow and slew it on the spot.

Zal was so impressed by this first success that he charged the youth with a task which would test his ability to command a small post. There was a stronghold atop Mount Sipand, where the growth of grain was luxuriant and water, game, and gold were in abundance. Only one approach up the mountain was possible, and that was carefully protected. Years before, the mighty hero Nariman had been killed trying to penetrate these defenses, and since then none dared to make the attempt. Now, although this kingdom had everything else in quantity, it lacked salt and prized this commodity very highly. Rustam, dressed as a salt merchant, went with a small caravan. In the city he was feted and received into the palace of the ruler. During the night Rustam led his men in an attack on the palace, overcame the guards, and captured the citadel. The choicest prizes from the treasury were sent to Zal, and, with the final destruction of the fortress, Nariman's death was avenged. Rustam's fame now began to spread throughout the land as the true heir of the mighty and noble Sam.

In the next few years, Iran suffered many reversals under the ineffectual rule of the last Pishdadian shahs. The Turanians were becoming such a threat on her borders that only the decisive leadership of a new and vigorous dynastic rule could prevent certain disaster. Zal enlisted Rustam's aid in this endeavor. He gave the youth Sam's mace and the choice of a horse from among his vast herds. The normal Arabian steed being too small, Rustam looked for a horse whose size and strength would correspond to his own. He inspected a great number until he was finally attracted to a piebald colt standing next to his mare. The herdsman gave the colt's name as "Rustam's Rakhsh" and told Rustam that no one dared to lasso it for fear of the mare's lion-like temper. When the youthful hero approached, the mare attacked him "like a furious elephant." Rustam let out a deafening roar, stunned her with fright and, with a powerful belt, thus sent her trembling back to the herd. He then mounted Rakhsh, "observed his courage, strength and blood," and was satisfied that he had made the right choice.

Thus all was made ready for war with the Turanians. The opposing armies were still two leagues apart when Zal declared that a new shah had to be crowned before going into battle. The high priests gave him the name of Kai Kubad as the lawful successor to the throne and first shah of the Kaianian dynasty. Because Kai Kubad lived a great distance away on Mount Elburz, Rustam was given a small company of men to find and escort the shah-elect back to his armies. On his way, Rustam was met by an outpost of Turanians whom he easily defeated. As they approached their destination, the Iranians stopped in an oasis and were surprised to find a young prince resting there with his attendants. The prince was Kai Kubad himself. He had seen two white hawks flying from Iran, carrying a crown as bright as the sun. Knowing from this vision that a messenger was bearing him extraordinary news, the prince had descended from his mountain palace to await the fateful herald in the oasis.

Kai Kubad was delighted to see Rustam and rejoiced in having been chosen to lead Iran against the Turanian invader. The return journey was interrupted by another Turkman band which had been sent by Afrasiyab to prevent the shah's reaching his troops. The fierce warrior, Kulun, who commanded this contingent, charged straight into Rustam and pierced his mail. But while the Turkman was exulting in his initial success, Rustam . . .

Seized on the spear and wrenched it from Kulun,
Then roared like thunder from the mountain tops,
Speared him and having raised him from his seat
Put the spear's but to the ground, Kulun
Was like a spitted bird in the sight of all.
The victor rode Rakhsh over him, and trod him
To death. . . .

When at last they rejoined Zal, Kai Kubad was crowned shah of Iran before all his paladins, surrounded on all sides by his cheering armies. Renewed in spirit, the Iranians set off under young Rustam's command, to meet the Turkman foe.

Waiting to open hostilities, the opposing forces carpeted the desert as far as the eye could see. Then they swarmed at one another in such massive waves that the dust they raised blackened the sky and the thundering beat of hoof and drum would have toppled great mountains. In the midst of battle Rustam asked Zal to point out Afrasiyab and rushed off to take the evil prince captive. Afrasiyab saw Rustam heading directly his way. He wondered in astonishment at "this dragon broken loose" and flew at him, thinking he could easily strike the youth down. As the Turanian prince closed in, Rustam reached out and snatched him up into the air. While in mid-air, Afrasiyab's belt snapped and he plummeted to the ground, thus narrowly escaping Rustam's clutches (Figure 2). Afrasiyab fled to his father, leaving the desert battle-ground stained a deep red hue from the blood of his slaughtered troops. Rustam alone had killed "eight hundred and fifty score of gallant chiefs" until the demoralized Turkmen finally retreated en masse "a trumpetless drumless lot."

Completely humiliated by his defeat, Afrasiyab described the young hero to his father . . .

"Thou know'st how kingly are my heart and hand,
My prowess, deeds, and enterprise, yet I
Am but a fibre in his grasp. Such worship
Perturbeth me. I saw a monstrous form
With lion's claws. My wits and senses fled.
Hill, cave, and level road were one to him
When his mad elephant was put to speed.
A thousand maces in good sooth and more
Fell on his famous helm: thou wouldst have said:
'They fashioned him of iron, brought him up
On stones and brass!' What is a sea or a mountain,
Fierce lion or mad elephant to him?"

Following this victory, the shah granted Rustam lands between Zabul and the Indus to rule as a vassal. Kai Kubad made his capital at Istakr and when he had put Iran into good order left the throne to his son, Kai Kaus.

At the very outset of Kai Kaus' reign, Firdausi intrudes upon the narrative to express critical disapproval of him and to apologize on behalf of Kai Kubad, "the noble tree," for having given life to "an evil shoot." Throughout the 150 years he ruled Iran, he often succumbed to the temptations of the

Figure 2. Rustam Snatches Afrasiyab from the Saddle
Safavid, dated A.H. 1020 (1618–19). Size of miniature: 6 1/2" × 6 1/4"
Courtesy of the Walters Art Gallery, Baltimore

devil and would yield to impulse, simply to suit his fancy, without giving thought to possible consequences. Kai Kaus ventured into his first war as a result of Ahriman's plotting. A *div* disguised as a minstrel entertained the shah with a beguiling song about the wondrous land of Mazandaran. Although he knew it was a land of *divs* and sorcerers, the shah was captivated by the prospect of adding this rich territory to his realm and ordered a large force prepared for the invasion. Thus despite anything Zal and all of Iran's greatest generals could say to stop him, Kai Kaus set off for Mazandaran, destroying cities and massacring populations along the way. The king of Mazandaran, incensed by the devastation of his lands, struck back and took the entire Iranian force, including the shah, prisoner. It was now up to Rustam to accomplish the near-impossible task of setting them free.

Two roads led to Mazandaran: one was the long way taken by the Iranians, and the second a fortnight's journey through extremely dangerous territory. Rustam's adventures on the road to Mazandaran are told as a series of seven courses, or trials, over which he had to triumph in order to save the shah and prove himself an undisputed hero.

During his first trial Rustam travelled at great speed, covering two days' journey in one day. Prostrate with fatigue and hunger, he and Rakhsh stopped at an oasis for the night. Rustam roasted an onager (a kind of wild ass) and then, turning Rakhsh loose to graze, fell to sleep on a bed of reeds. A lion passing nearby decided to kill the horse first and then feed upon Rustam. When he attacked, however, Rakhsh flew at him, dug his teeth into the lion's back, and dashed him to pieces. The commotion roused Rustam from his sleep and, seeing the remains of the lion, scolded the horse for having taken so great a risk on his own.

The next day they came to a desert where the sun's intense heat parched the earth and made both horse and master limp with thirst and fatigue. Rustam fell to the ground exhausted and prayed for God's help. All at once a well-fed ram appeared, led Rustam to a watering place, and then vanished. Giving thanks to Hormuzd for this divine messenger, Rustam refreshed himself and rested. Before going to sleep, however, he warned Rakhsh to make no friends and to fight with no one alone. It happened that they were in the haunt of a dragon, who appeared shortly after Rustam had fallen asleep. The beast attacked Rakhsh twice but hid out of sight before the horse could awaken his master. Rustam, suspecting Rakhsh of playing pranks, threatened to behead him if this should happen again. On the third attack, Rakhsh hesitated at first but then jolted Rustam out of his slumber. This time Rustam saw the raging monster and slew it with his sword.

The following day they travelled on for a long time and came to rest in a lovely shaded spot. Beside a sparkling stream, Rustam saw a freshly roasted sheep, bread, sweetmeats, and a golden bowl filled with wine. This oasis belonged to sorcerers who had withdrawn into hiding when they saw Rustam approach. One of the witches turned herself into a beautiful young girl and appeared before the hero to join him in making merry. As he offered her a cup of wine, invoking the name of God, she immediately turned back into a wrinkled hag, and Rustam struck her down, thus making "the hearts of sorcerers afraid." The last three of Rustam's trials are covered in the text facing Plate I.

Once released from captivity, Kai Kaus was determined to pursue the total submission of Mazandaran. He sent Rustam as emissary, but the king refused to submit and foolishly tried to put Rustam to death. The hero escaped from his captors, then led the angered Iranians to take Mazandaran by force. In order to elude Rustam's lasso the king, being a sorcerer, transformed himself into stone. Not to be outdone by trickery, Rustam carried the heavy rock back to his camp and waited until the king, believing himself out of danger, returned to flesh. The moment this happened, Rustam pounced on him and cut him to pieces.

Kai Kaus felt himself sufficiently avenged with the defeat of Mazandaran but it was not long before he embarked upon wars with other neighboring states. He exacted tribute from Hamaravan and took the king's daughter, Sudaba, for his wife. Her father was so enraged that he tricked Kai Kaus and Sudaba into his palace and had them thrown into prison. Once again Turan took advantage of the shah's absence, invaded Iran, and placed Afrasiyab upon the Iranian throne. Rustam gathered a large army out of Zabul, Kabul, and Hindustan, defeated Hamaravan, and then routed the Turkmen out of Iran.

The experiences of Mazandaran and Hamaravan began to have some effect upon Kai Kaus. He stayed out of disputes with his neighbors and put his realm into order. But then one day, to everyone's amazement, the shah ascended into the sky. The evil Iblis, wishing to disgrace him, sent a *div* in disguise to propose that the shah fly to the moon and stars and proclaim them part of his lawful realm. He ascended on a throne tied to four eagles but, eventually, this primitive flying-machine broke down. The eagles grew tired and fell back to earth delivering Kai Kaus into the hands of the *divs*. Rustam led a host of the shah's greatest paladins to the rescue, and Kai Kaus spent forty days in solitude praying for the Almighty to forgive his vanity and greed. Since it now appeared that the shah had learned his lesson and Iran might enjoy some peace, Rustam went off to hunt some game. At this time he found his way to the Turanian kingdom of Samangan where he met the princess Tahminah. From their marriage was born a son, Suhrab, whose story is told in the text facing Plates II and III.

A few years later Rustam took Siyawush, the child of Kai Kaus, to raise as his own son. The prince later suffered so much abuse from the shah that he went into the service of Turan, where he greatly distinguished himself and married Afrasiyab's daughter, Ferengis. His successes aroused the envy of a Turkman chief and, one night, Siyawush was surreptitiously put to death. Ferengis gave birth to Kai Khusrau, the next shah of Iran, chosen while still a youth to rule in partnership with the aging Kai Kaus. Iran had been losing much of her former strength under the old shah and now that Khusrau was assuming leadership recovery was in prospect. Embassies from all over the world came to do him homage and foremost among them were his most trusted friends, Zal and Rustam.

When tidings reached the Shah: "The loyal Rustam
Is on his way," the people as one man
Arose to go to welcome him.
The Shah was glad and bade the courier: "Take
Thy pleasure here, for Rustam reared my father,
And all eyes recognize his excellence."

As soon as Rustam's standard came in sight,
And when the host's dust mounted o'er the sun,
Shouts rose with sound of trump and kettledrum,
And from the center Giv, Gudarz, and Tus
Approached in haste the elephantine chieftain,
And gave him salutations joyfully . . .

. . . Now when Khusrau
Beheld the elephantine warrior
Tears trickled from his eyelids down his cheeks.
Descending from the throne he greeted Rustam,
Who kissed the ground. The Shah said: "Paladin!
Live ever glad and be happy, for thou art
The foster-sire of Siyawush and likewise
Art of all men most wise and reticent."
He clasped upon his breast the head of Zal,
And sorrowed for his own sire's sake the while,
Then seated both his chiefs on the royal throne,
And blessed them in God's name . . .

Kai Khusrau promised his retiring grandfather that the murder of Siyawush would be avenged. He sent his captain, Tus, with a host into Turan, but this expedition was defeated and finally beseiged atop Mount Hamawan. Rustam was dispatched with an army to reinforce them, while Afrasiyab engaged the services of Kamus, a mighty warrior from Kashan, and the khan of Chin.

The tents and tent-enclosures filled the world
With red and yellow, blue and violet.
Amidmost each enclosure was a standard
Wrought of brocade of Chin and painted silk.
He[4] stood amazed and asked himself in wonder:
"Is this a paradise, or banquet-hall,
The starry heaven, or orbit of the moon?"

The Turkman leaders planned an attack which they thought would annihilate the isolated Iranians. The contending forces were drawn up just as Rustam arrived to relieve the Iranian army. The warrior Ashkabus "whose voice was like a kettledrum" made the initial challenge and was slain in a fight with Rustam (Plate IV). Then the two armies fell upon one another. Rustam killed the chieftain Kamus, and, despite the Turanians' efforts to call a truce, the victors pushed further into their lines of defense. Rustam lassoed their chiefs, while Tus and other paladins followed to take them captive. The terrified khan of Chin, in an effort to dissociate himself from Afrasiyab, sent a message to Rustam . . .

"Fight not so fiercely.
These troops of Chin, of Shakn, Changhan and Wahr
Have in their hearts no interest in the feud,
Nor have the kings of Chin and of Khatlan.
[4] Piran, commander of the Turanian forces.

Thou hast no quarrel with these aliens,
But with Afrasiyab, who knoweth not
The fire from water, but hath raised the world,
And by this war brought evil on himself.
We all of us have greed and long for fame,
Yet peace still bettereth war."

The messenger made overtures of conciliation on behalf of the khan but succeeded only in angering Rustam all the more. He forged ahead, taking many more prisoners until he came to the khan himself. In a desperate effort to fight Rustam off, the khan threw a sharp ax at his assailant but failed to hit him. Rustam then flung his lasso. He caught the khan by the neck, dragged him off his elephant down to the ground. With Kamus dead and the khan taken prisoner, the Turanians now fell back in panic and defeat. Rustam pressed on still more hoping to capture Afrasiyab, but once again the infamous prince eluded him. The shah was well satisfied with this victory, and Rustam's return to Iran was an occasion of great rejoicing. A lavish feast was held in his honor, and Kai Khusrau rewarded him generously for bringing this nearly disastrous campaign to a successful conclusion (Plate V).

Following this war, Rustam met with an adventure occasioned by the marriage of the young Iranian paladin, Bizhan, to Afrasiyab's daughter, Manizha (Figure 1). Her angered father had Bizhan thrown into a deep pit covered over by a heavy boulder so that the youth would starve to death. Manizha was banished from Turan but she stole back to her husband and kept him alive by dropping food to him through a small hole. Rustam, disguised as a merchant, passed unnoticed into Turan, lifted the tremendous weight of the boulder unaided, and rescued Bizhan.

Now fully determined to defeat his arch-foe Kai Khusrau waged a great war against Afrasiyab. After suffering two crushing defeats Afrasiyab again managed to escape into the mountains. He took refuge in a cave where a holy man discovered him and delivered him up to the shah. Finally, in the name of all the gallant Iranians he had slain and in revenge for the evil he had brought upon the world, Khusrau took Afrasiyab and cut him in two at the waist. Having lived only for this day of reckoning, Kai Kaus now died, and Khusrau reigned alone for another sixty years in peace and prosperity. But the

shah began to weary of the world. Having decided to quit life on earth, he chose his son, Luhrasp, as his successor and made ready to pass without death into Paradise. The day this miracle occurred, Rustam and all the great paladins followed their monarch to a mountain top where five of them waited until Kai Khusrau vanished from sight.[5]

Luhrasp reigned for 120 years and reluctantly resigned the throne to his son Gushtasp. One of Gushtasp's sons, Isfandiyar, proved himself a hero with a series of seven exploits similar to Rustam's trials. Isfandiyar asked his father to relinquish the crown, but rather than step down, Gushtasp plotted his son's death.[6] A high priest predicted that the prince was fated to be killed by Rustam, and so Gushtasp sought an opportunity to have the two meet as adversaries. Finding his excuse in Rustam's infrequent visits to court, the shah pretended to have taken offense by this and promised to give Isfandiyar the throne when he should bring Rustam back in chains.

Suspecting nothing of this evil design, Isfandiyar dutifully set upon taking Rustam captive. When he reached Sistan, Rustam's native province, the prince sent his son, Bahman, with a message announcing the shah's will. Rustam, though defiant, could hardly believe Isfandiyar would come to him with such a demand. He invited the prince and his company to stay six months as his guests, settle the problem peacefully, and then, if he wished to return to Gushtasp . . .

"I will not separate my reins from thine,
And we will go to him in company.
By asking pardon I will soothe his wrath,
And kiss him on the head and feet and eyes.
Then will I ask the great but unjust Shah:
'Why should these hands of mine be put in bonds?'"

Isfandiyar would not yield. Rustam, despite his life-long pledge of loyalty to the shah, refused to submit to such an indignity and the clash of convictions touched off the celebrated combat which was to end with the death of Isfandiyar (Plates VII and VIII).

Rustam kept Bahman, as he had Siyawush, to train in preparation for the throne. He wrote to Gushtasp with an explanation of his efforts to make peace with Isfandiyar, requesting the shah's pledge to take no revenge. With royal pardon given, Rustam felt released from his burden of guilt and

[5] See text to Plate VI. [6] See text to Plate VII.

returned Bahman to his grandfather unaware that the prince would one day turn upon the house of Zal. In some versions of this story it was Bahman who finally did Rustam in. Firdausi, however, chose another course.

Rustam had a half-brother, Shaghad, who was sent for his early training to the kingdom of Kabul. Under the king's tutelage Shaghad developed into an astute and skillful chieftain. Because he was a vassal to Zal, the king gave one of his daughters to Shaghad, hoping through this marriage to effect the cancellation of tribute. When the next payment was accepted, however, Shaghad and the king plotted Rustam's death. They planned a feast during which the king would insult Shaghad before witnesses. The youth would take his grievance to Zal and then, surely, Rustam would be sent to demand retribution. Knowing of Rustam's love for the hunt, ten large pits were dug in the grounds about Kabul and in them were planted long, sharp spear points. When the Iranians reached the gates of Kabul, the king threw himself at Rustam's feet, begging for his mercy. Remembering his gratitude to the king for having raised Shaghad, Rustam was pacified and Kabul spared. Then, at the king's invitations, he went out to the hunting grounds to enjoy the chase, and the villainy of the plotters was concluded. By the end of that fateful day Rustam had ridden to his doom, a victim of ambition and greed. To a stunned Iran, the death of Rustam marked the end of a fabulous era. The news of Rustam's death spread quickly and a great cry of anguish resounded throughout the land.

They requisitioned roses, musk and wine.
The man who sewed the shroud shed tears of blood
On combing out that beard of camphor hue.
Two strechers scarce sufficed to hold the body;
Was it a man's trunk or a shady tree's?
They fashioned out of teak a goodly coffin
With golden nails and ivory ornaments.
The apertures were all sealed up with pitch,
Which they o'erlaid with musk and spicery.

Mourning was universal, and the funeral procession, the most spectacular ever known (Plate IX).

Here the poet, aging and all too aware of life's impermanence, adds a final word, likening the world to a temporary resting-place where the wayfarer stays a while and then departs . . .

What wouldst thou with this Wayside Inn – this gain
Of treasure first but in the end of pain?
Serve God or Ahriman yet still thou must,
Though made of iron, crumble into dust,
Yet lean to good while here thou shalt abide,
Elsewhere perchance thou wilt be satisfied.

Rustam Fights the White Div of Mazandaran

Persian-Mongol School, 14th century
Size of miniature: 1 3/4" × 4 1/4"
Courtesy of the Cincinnati Art Museum

THE SHAH and his armies were imprisoned by sorcerers in the kingdom of Mazandaran. On the way to liberate them, Rustam survived encounters with a lion, a dragon, and a witch.[1] Then he passed through a region of darkness, finally emerging into a bright and fertile country. Here he took captive the prince, Ulad, who consented to guide Rustam safely through the rest of his perilous journey.

Further along the road, Rustam sought the *div*, Arzhang, a fearful demon who protected Mazandaran from attack. Finding the *div* at his cave, Rustam overcame the monster, wrenched off its head and hurled it at the terrified demon guards. Now safely arrived at the citadel Rustam and Ulad reached the Iranians only to find all of them blind from the humiliation and grief of their defeat. Recovery was possible only by having the magic blood from the White Div, an even more horrible creature than Arzhang, dropped into their eyes.

Rustam crossed even mountains to get to the White Div's cavern. Once there, Ulad advised him not to attack until the hottest part of the day, when all the guards would be asleep. At the appointed hour, Rustam tied Ulad to a tree and slipped into the cave. He wandered through long dark passages eventually coming upon the great white beast. The hero rushed at the demon and they fell into a savage struggle, tearing into one another's flesh until the ground was drenched with their blood. Hours passed before Rustam could throw his opponent. Swiftly then, he plunged his dagger into the *div*'s heart and cut out his liver. It was with the blood of this liver that Rustam was able to cure the Iranians of their blindness and thus restore Kai Kaus to his throne.

Taken from one of the small *Shahnamas* of the Il-Khanid period, this painting shows how the characteristically Iranian patterning of form and color persisted despite the current interest in finely brushed line. The battle is presented through a cut-away view of the cave, focusing attention upon Rustam and the *div* with its fantastically horned, lion-like face. As though a performer on stage acknowledging the admiration and applause of his audience, the hero strikes a pose of victory. He wears a Mongol-type helmet and the tiger-skin cuirass, by which he is identified, over a richly brocaded Persian garment. The amazed onlooker peering over the rocks negates the separation between the interior of the cave and the out-of-doors, where Rakhsh and Ulad, bound to a tree, wait for Rustam. The color, though rich, is sparingly used in patterns of blue, green, and red so arranged as to give this painting its quality of gold inset with precious stones.

[1] See page 10 of Introduction.

Tahminah Comes to Rustam's Chamber

Timurid, between 1409 and 1415
Size of miniature: 7 7/8" × 4"
Courtesy of the Fogg Art Museum, Harvard University

DURING an interval of peace, Rustam went out to hunt on the plains of Turan. One evening, after the day's chase was done, he lay down to nap as Rakhsh grazed nearby. A passing band of Turanians abducted the horse to the kingdom of Samangan. Upon awakening, the hero's search for Rakhsh took him to that city, where the king entertained him lavishly and gave him comfortable quarters for the night.

In the middle of the night Rustam was awakened by whispering outside his door. As the curtain was raised he saw a servant enter carrying a candle that lighted the face of another person – a beautiful young girl. She was Tahminah, the king's daughter who for years had rejected all suitors hoping that some day Rustam might come. If he would have her, Tahminah promised to return the horse and to put all of Samangan at his feet. Rustam was captivated by her charm, and they were married the next day. He departed the following morning, however, leaving his armlet as a token. Should their child be a girl Tahminah was to plait it in her hair and if a boy she was to bind it round his arm.

Tahminah gave birth to Suhrab, who, by the age of ten was as big and powerful as his father. Anxious for the boy's well-being, Tahminah concealed his father's identity. But after persistent questioning, Suhrab persuaded her to reveal her secret. Thus as Tahminah had feared, the impulsive youth gathered an army declaring his intention to depose the unworthy Kaus and to crown Rustam shah of Iran.

One of the great romantic episodes of the *Shahnama*, Tahminah's meeting with Rustam is shown here in an outstanding example of Timurid painting style. In this high, elegant chamber all is told in delicate adjustments of pattern and space. The slender height of Taminah is repeated in the long lines of the windows and door, while the curve of the curtain enhances the grace of her gesture. With head tilted to one side she demurely hides part of her face with her mantle. Rustam, reclining, props up his head and gazes eagerly in anticipation of her approach.

The deep tones of color invite the suggestion of darkness in the chamber which now functions as a fully developed architectural background with integrated perspective levels. These elements, plus the mastery of technique and the size of the painting, indicate that the painter had now won a place equal to the calligrapher as creator of the art of the book.

Rustam Recognizes the Dead Suhrab

Safavid, dated 1618–19
Size of miniature: 7 1/4″ × 5 1/4″
Courtesy of the Walters Art Gallery, Baltimore

SUHRAB's fame spread as he marched to Iran. A description of him aroused Rustam's curiosity; the thought that this might be Tahminah's son crossed his mind but was quickly dismissed.

One night, as the two armies massed on the plain, Rustam stole behind the enemy line disguised as a Turkman. The sight of the mighty youth confirmed all advance reports. Though Suhrab looked distinctly Iranian, Rustam still failed to recognize him as his son. On the battlefield the next morning, Suhrab, though defiant of Rustam's threats, asked in a friendly tone if he were not addressing the famous hero. The father rebuffed this advance as impertinent and replied that he was not.

They chose a battleground and fought, first with javelins, then with scimitars and last with maces until dark, continuing the next day with a wrestling match. That night Suhrab overcame Rustam. As he drew his sword, Rustam protested that Iranian rules of combat forbid the victor to deliver the death blow until he has thrown his adversary twice. In a magnanimous gesture, Suhrab let him go.

Running off into the hills alone, Rustam prayed to God to restore the strength which, years before, he had asked to be diminished. In the following day's struggle each was bent upon the other's destruction, but Suhrab was unequal to Rustam's full power. The hero threw him to the ground and stabbed him in the chest. As he lay dying, Suhrab confessed his failure to join forces with Rustam, his father. Now recognizing the armlet, and half-crazed by this revelation, Rustam tried to decapitate himself but was restrained by his comrades. He hastened to get a special elixir from Kai Kaus; a messenger however overtook the wretched father with word that Suhrab had died.

This miniature reflects the style of the late Safavid period, which retains the small scale and brilliant color of the early 16th century. Generally elegant and mannered, this style was characterized by frequent use of curved line and attenuated form (Plate V). Rustam, in the center, wears his tiger-skin cuirass and a high headdress of a leopard's mask. The diagonal line of Suhrab's body is carried up by the broad curve of the tree into the outer sky, suggesting his soul's flight to Paradise. Peering over the hill, a group of spectators are given the conventional gesture of finger held to lips to express astonishment. Except for the two horses, the center space is cleared to give full view and greater dramatic impact to one of the most touching episodes of the *Shahnama*.

Rustam Slays Ashkabus and His Horse

Mongol period, Inju dynasty, Shiraz. 14th century
Size of miniature: 3 5/16" × 6"
Courtesy of the Smithsonian Institution, Freer Gallery of Art, Washington, D.C.

IRAN WAS at war with the forces of Turan and Chin (China).[1] As the opposing armies took up their positions, Ashkabus, a Turkman warrior from Kashan, rode to the front hurling defiance at the Iranians. Rustam went out on foot to meet this insolent challenge and, after a prolonged exchange of threats and warnings, struck his opponent's horse with an arrow. The steed fell forward, pitching his master to the ground. Recovering swiftly, the Turkman discharged a shower of arrows but failed to pierce the hero's armor. Then Rustam took a single poplar shaft, put it to the deerhide bowstring and sent it straight into the breast of Ashkabus.

> *. . . the sky kissed Rustam's hand;*
> *Then destiny cried: "Take!" and fate cried: "Give!"*
> *The heavens cried: "Excellent!" the angels: "Good!"*
> *He of Kashan expired, thou wouldst have said:*
> *"His mother never bare him!"*

Unaware that Rustam was the one who stepped out to answer Ashkabus, the Turanian generals were shocked to see their invincible chieftain dispatched so quickly. Here began the demoralization of the Turanians that was to be their ultimate defeat.

The miniature of Rustam slaying Ashkabus represents a style that prevailed under the Inju rulers of Shiraz in the 14th century. Whereas contemporary Il-Khanid painting of Tabriz and Baghdad is marked by an influence from China (Plates I and VIII), that of Shiraz has a distinctly archaic quality recalling the decorative arts of the Saljuks (Figure 1). It has been suggested that the character of Inju art stemmed from a mural-painting tradition adapted to book illustration, the same artists perhaps working in both media.[2] Thin earth pigments are applied to designs, which have been found particularly suitable to certain architectural features of that area. In this painting the colors are limited to earth ochres, green, and red, bounded by a spirited black line. Landscape is suggested in the simple band of cross-hatching that serves as a ground plane, and by the fantastic bold flowers which fill the plain, white background.

The incident is expressed in vigorous plays of line, form, and negative spaces. At the right, where Rustam has just let fly his arrow, both the hero and the plants are standing vertically. As the foliage bends further to the left with increasing animation it directs the gaze to Ashkabus and augments the movement of his falling body.

[1] See page 11 of Introduction.
[2] Eric Schroeder: *Persian Miniatures in the Fogg Museum of Art*, Cambridge, 1942

20

Kai Khusrau Feasts Rustam

Safavid, dated A.H. 1020 (1618–19)
Size of miniature: 8″ × 5″
Courtesy of the Walters Art Gallery, Baltimore

A WARM relationship always existed between Rustam and Kai Khusrau. The greatest force binding them was their mutual devotion to the memory of Khusrau's father, Siyawush, whom Rustam had brought up as his own son. The shah's wise and enlightened rule, in contrast to that of the foolish Kaus, appealed to Rustam's strong sense of justice. Furthermore, both men shared an insatiable drive to do away with Iran's most deadly foe, Afrasiyab, and thereby avenge the murder of Siyawush.

Kai Khusrau here honors Rustam for his most recent victory in the great war with the Turanians and the khan of Chin. The Iranian forces had been besieged on a mountain and would have been completely annihilated had Rustam not arrived in time to take command and throw the enemy back. Now at the peak of their careers, the two men meet as devoted friends as well as king and subject.

This scene takes place before the shah's throne, which is abstracted into a flat backdrop rather than shown as a spatial enclosure. The tops of two cypress trees project above the architecture and even protrude beyond the picture border into the margin of the page. These are undoubtedly references to the two protagonists, recalling Firdausi's frequent allusions to the cypress as simile for a tall, strong, and graceful youth. Above the throne two Simurg birds are placed in heraldic fashion symbolizing power and divine protection over the shah of Iran.

The scale of pictorial elements and the color, now radically changed from those of the 14th century, are in the tradition of early-16th-century Safavid painting. Brilliant reds, blues, yellows, and greens are brought into harmony with an array of softer pastel tones. The figures are drawn in the style favored during the reign of Shah Abbas I. Their bodies tend to be elongated and the heads proportionately small. They stand in such a way that the contour of the entire figure sweeps into a curve. This style, originated by painters of the late 16th century, was carried into the 17th century by Riza-i-Abbasi and came into such favor that it continued, much degenerated, into the 18th century. The large turbans worn here were fashionable at the end of the 16th century and are rendered in the manner of Riza, with all folds clearly indicated in swift calligraphic brush strokes.

Rustam and the Iranians in the Snow

Signed by Mu'in Musavvir, probably Isfahan, about 1640
Size of miniature: 13 3/4" × 8 1/16"
Courtesy of the Fogg Art Museum, Harvard University

KAI KHUSRAU achieved the climax of his reign when he captured and put the infamous Afrasiyab to death. In his remaining sixty years, peaceful though they were, he fell into a state of melancholy and finally withdrew entirely from life at court.

One night after having prayed to be taken from this world, the shah had a dream in which the angel Surush appeared. Through his vision Kai Khusrau was told that the Almighty had set aside a place for him in heaven. He was to settle his affairs on earth and enter into Paradise. This decision distressed all Iran yet even Rustam and Zal could not induce the shah to change his mind. Finally, bidding all farewell, Kai Khusrau made a long journey up to a mountain, accompanied by Zal, Rustam, and six other paladins, while thousands of his grieving subjects lined the road.

Having reached the mountain top, the shah urged his captains to turn back. Rustam, Zal, and Gudarz reluctantly departed but the rest chose to remain with their king up to his last moment on earth. That night Kai Khusrau walked away from his paladins, reciting the *Zend-Avesta*[1] as he went, and vanished from sight. A blizzard struck the mountain, and the five who had stayed behind perished under the mounting snows. The next day Rustam, Zal, and Gudarz went back to the mountain. They searched everywhere in vain for their comrades and, as we see in this miniature, waited patiently long hours for a sign of life.

A comparison with the two other 17th-century paintings of Plates III and V shows how few Safavid conventions are retained here. Mu'in Musavvir, one of the finest painters of this period, organized this picture somewhat in the 14th-century manner, but with a freshness of style of his own. The forms are large within the picture area; they are rendered with simplicity and, except for the parasols, have little surface embellishment. The paladins loom over the mountain top, far out of scale with the landscape. Foreign influences are seen in the Chinese character of the rocks and in the Western style of rendering the stormy sky. Little of the intense Safavid color remains. Instead, the more limited palette, dominated by closely related violets and blues, helps to sustain the sorrowful mood that is projected by the faces and gestures of the figures. Below them the horses wait expectantly, facing the snowdrifts that show the banners of the doomed paladins.

[1] Zoroastrian holy scriptures.

24

The Battle of Rustam and Isfandiyar

Persian-Mongol School, probably from Tabriz, about the mid-14th century
Size of miniature: 6 3/8" × 11 1/2"
Courtesy of the William Rockhill Nelson Gallery of Art, Kansas City, Missouri

SHAH GUSHTASP plotted his son's death by promising to give him the throne on the condition that he put Rustam into chains. The prince, Isfandiyar, innocently went off to execute his father's wish. He found, however, that it would not be simply done.[1] Rustam was willing to go before the shah . . .

> *"And do whate'er thou biddest save these bonds,*
> *For they are utter shame, defeat and outrage.*
> *No one shall see me bound while I survive . . ."*

All of Rustam's efforts to make the prince see through this plot were to no avail, for Isfandiyar denied Gushtasp's treachery and challenged Rustam to fight the next morning.

When they met on the battlefield, each ordered his troops to stay behind and not give battle. The two paladins fell into an earth-shaking struggle; they used javelins until they broke, then scimitars as seen in this miniature, and then without weapons they tugged at one another trying to unseat the adversary. While the leaders fought, Rustam's brothers disregarded their pledge to stand by and led an attack upon the opposition, killing two of Isfandiyar's sons. Although condemned by Rustam, this action so infuriated Isfandiyar that he dispatched a shower of arrows that sent Rustam and Rakhsh flying home to nurse their wounds. When Zal saw his grievously wounded son he called for aid from the fabulous bird Simurg.[2]

This battle scene represents one of the several painting styles employed in the "Demotte" *Shahnama*.[3] The protagonists are shown rushing at one another brandishing their scimitars, the horses plunging into the air at a flying gallop.

The symmetrical arrangement of the figures creates an open space in the center of the picture. However, instead of remaining static, this area is highly charged by the sweeping curves of the horses, whose heads are at the very point of clashing. Although some defiance is expressed in the men's faces, they appear quite restrained compared to the fierce look of the horses. The color, predominantly in tones of reddish-browns and blues, is, in its present state, entirely subordinated to the action of the line. Originally painted in silver, the weapons have blackened with age, and, since the paint of the armor is almost gone, the tonal relationships are now changed. A relatively slight Chinese influence is noted in the bare landscape. Reduced to simple converging lines, the background suggests an open desert beyond the limits of the picture. In this stark setting, the figures emerge very large against the sky, where a few Chinese clouds, with flame-like tentacles, hint at the impending violence.

[1] See page 12 of Introduction.　[2] See page 6 of Introduction.　[3] See page 4 of Introduction.

Rustam Slays Isfandiyar

Persian-Mongol School, probably Tabriz, about the mid-14th century
Size of miniature: 7 3/8″ × 11 1/4″
E. W. Forbes Collection, courtesy of the Fogg Art Museum, Harvard University

ZAL'S HEAVENLY protector, the fabulous bird Simurg, healed Rustam's wounds and revealed heaven's decree that the slayer of Isfandiyar would himself be pursued by anguish the rest of his life. She urged him to settle his dispute without bloodshed but, on the other hand, showed Rustam how the prince could be slain. Taking him to a tamarisk tree, the wood destined to be fatal to Isfandiyar, the Simurg prescribed the way to make the deadly arrow. With his weapon made, Rustam went on to meet Isfandiyar, hoping he would not have to resort to its use. He offered the prince riches and even consented to go to the shah, unbound, though he might later be put into chains. Isfandiyar rebuffed this compromise with the charge that Zal had used sorcery to heal Rustam's wounds. For the last time Rustam pleaded his cause but Isfandiyar stayed his ground. Rustam, he declared, would have him go against the wishes of the shah and, therefore, of God.

> "... O famous Rustam!
> Thy soul is satiate of fight, but now
> Thou shalt behold the arrows of Gushtasp ..."

As the prince delivered his last threat, all hope vanished and Rustam strung up his bow. The shaft of tamarisk cut through the air and struck Isfandiyar between the eyes.

The prince dropped his bow, clutched his horse's mane as he fell forward and catapulted to the ground. The earth turned red where Isfandiyar lay but he sat up and pulled the arrow from his head. He knew at once this was the arrow sent by the Simurg and realized that Rustam's death blow was destiny's reply to greed and treachery. Finally he gasped, "This wrong hath come upon me from Gushtasp," and died.

This, another leaf from the "Demotte" *Shahnama*, may be compared with the example of Plate VII. Chinese elements are more apparent in the work of this artist, notably in the scroll clouds, the jagged non-symmetrical trees, and in the use of graded tone. The figures are again placed almost equidistant from the center, large in scale but surrounded by a far more complex landscape.

The text is followed closely. Dramatic effect is gained by the contrast between Rustam's mighty gesture and the limp figure of Isfandiyar. The violence expressed in the shattered foreground trees and approaching storm is intensified by the rich blue in the sky, while the fresh color of the flowers add a note of irony. A group of deer, startled by the storm, further emphasize the image of sudden and senseless turmoil descending upon the peaceful order of nature.

The Funeral of Rustam

Persian-Mongol School, probably Tabriz, about the mid-14th century
Size of miniature: 6 3/16" × 11 11/16"
Courtesy of the Museum of Fine Arts, Boston

A SCHEME to kill Rustam was succeeding.[1] The hero came to Kabul, settled a sham dispute peacefully, and rode out to the hunting grounds where deep pits had been secretly dug. When Rakhsh detected the smell of freshly dug earth he stopped short, and turned about, proceeding cautiously between the cleverly hidden pits. Thinking the horse's behavior strange, Rustam lashed him lightly just as he was trying to avoid one of the traps. Rakhsh stumbled and went down, taking Rustam with him.

> . . . all below was spear
> And sword; no pluck availed; escape was none;
> And so the haunches of the mighty Rakhsh,
> And Rustam's legs and bosom, were impaled;
> Yet in his manhood he uplifted him,
> And from the bottom bravely gained the brim.

As soon as Rustam saw the faces of his half-brother, Shaghad, and the king of Kabul, their treachery was clearly revealed. Fatally wounded, he asked his brother to string up his bow and put it within reach so that he might prevent lions from tearing him to pieces before death came. This Shaghad did and laughed for joy at his brother's fate. Upon seeing this ultimate villainy, Rustam summoned his last strength and grabbed his bow. Shaghad fled in terror to a plane tree and hid behind it, but Rustam's arrow hit its mark and Shaghad died instantly – pinned to that tree.

The news of Rustam's death spread rapidly. His wounds were sewn, his body washed and then wrapped in a shroud of the finest brocades. It took two days to draw the giant body of Rakhsh out of the pit and lay it on an elephant's back. All having been made ready, the splendid procession made its way slowly to Zabul, bearing Rustam on his final journey home.

> Kabulistan up to Zabulistan
> Was like a place of public lamentation,
> And men and women stood there in such throngs
> That none had room to move, and so they passed
> The coffins on from hand to hand and thought,
> Such were their multitudes, the travail wind.
> They reached Zabul in two days and a night,
> And neither bier was seen to touch the ground.

A great charnel house was built within a garden where all men, from the highest to the lowest ranks, gathered at the bier to pour roses and musk at Rustam's feet, and bid him a last farewell.

Rustam's funeral, another miniature from the "Demotte" *Shahnama*, is made by the

[1] See page 13 of Introduction.

same artist, or artists, who produced the example of Plate VII. The flat background permits all attention to concentrate upon the cortege which conveys a sense of continuing beyond the margin. Facial expressions and the unhurried movement of the mourners project a silent internal grief most vividly seen in the figure who bends under the immense weight of Rustam's bier. Color and pattern contribute toward the same effect. The figures are clothed in plain robes of black and dark tones of brown and blue. Against the lighter ground, these forms enhance the mood of melancholy, while the bulk of Rakhsh and the elephant dramatize the ponderous nature of the procession. Attention is given to individual characteristics such as facial types, hair coloring and differences in age. The old man at the right is probably Rustam's father, perhaps the only person who had known so intimately the glories and reversals of the hero's life.

SELECTED BIBLIOGRAPHY

T. W. Arnold: *Painting in Islam*, London, 1928

———: *Bihzad and His Paintings in the Zafar-namah MS*, London, 1930

——— and A. Grohmann: *The Islamic Book*, Paris, 1929

D. Barrett: *Persian Painting of the Fourteenth Century*, The Faber Gallery of Oriental Art, London, 1952

L. Binyon, J.V.S. Wilkinson, and Basil Gray: *Persian Miniature Painting*, Oxford, 1933

E. Blochet: *Musulman Painting*, London, 1929

D. Brian: "A Reconstruction of the Miniature Cycle in the Demotte *Shahnama*," *Ars Islamica*, VI, 2, Ann Arbor, 1939

Columbia University: *Firdausi Celebration*, 935-1935, New York, 1936

M. S. Dimand: *Mohammedan Decorative Arts*, New York Metropolitan Museum, 1930

B. Gray: *Persian Painting*, London, 1930

Iran: Early Persian Miniatures from the Imperial Library of the Shah of Iran at the Gulistan Palace, The UNESCO World Art Series, New York Graphic Society, 1956

F. R. Martin: *The Miniature Painting and Painters of Persia, India and Turkey*, London, 1912

J. Mohl: *Le Livre des Rois par Abou'l-Kasim Firdausi*, Paris, 1876

A. U. Pope and P. Ackerman, ed.: *A Survey of Persian Art*, Oxford, 1938

A. Sakisian: *La Miniature Persane*, Paris, 1929

E. Schroeder: *Persian Miniatures in the Fogg Museum of Art*, Cambridge, 1942

———: "Ahmad Musa and Shams al-Din, a Review of Fourteenth Century Painting," *Ars Islamica*, VI, 2, Ann Arbor, 1939

P. W. Schulz: *Die Persisch-Islamische Miniaturmalerai*, Leipzig, 1914

A. G. Warner and E. Warner: *The Shahnama of Firdausi*, London, 1905-25

J. V. S. Wilkinson: *The Shah-Nama of Firdausi*, London, 1931